ideals HOME

More Than 50 Years of Celebrating Life's Most Treasured Moments

Vol. 52, No. 5

"Stay, stay at home, my heart, and rest;
Home-keeping hearts are happiest."

—Henry Wadsworth Longfellow

IDEALS—Vol. 52, No. 5 August MCMXCV IDEALS (ISSN 0019-137X) is published eight times a year: February, March, May, June, August, September, November, December by IDEALS PUBLICATIONS INCORPORATED, 535 Metroplex Drive, Suite 250, Nashville, Tennessee 37211. Second-class postage paid at Nashville, Tennessee, and additional mailing offices. Copyright © MCMXCV by IDEALS PUBLICATIONS INCORPORATED. POSTMASTER: Send address changes to Ideals, P.O. Box 305300, Nashville, Tennessee 37230. All rights reserved. Title IDEALS registered U.S. Patent Office.

SINGLE ISSUE—U.S. $4.95 USD; Higher in Canada
ONE-YEAR SUBSCRIPTION—8 issues—U.S. $19.95 USD; Canada $36.00 CDN (incl. GST and shipping); Foreign $25.95 USD
TWO-YEAR SUBSCRIPTION—16 issues—U.S. $35.95 USD; Canada $66.50 CDN (incl. GST and shipping); Foreign $47.95 USD

Printed and bound in USA by The Banta Company, Menasha, Wisconsin. Printed on Weyerhaeuser Husky.

The paper used in this publication meets the minimum requirements of American National Standard for Information Sciences—Permanence of Paper for Printed Library Materials, ANSI Z39.48-1984.

Unsolicited manuscripts will not be returned without a self-addressed, stamped envelope.

ISBN 0-8249-1129-6   GST 131903775

Cover Photo GARDEN OF MAGNOLIA RIDGE PLANTATION
Washington, Louisiana, R Krubner/H. Armstrong Roberts

Inside Covers SEASIDE GARDEN. Eleanor Lane, Artist,
under license of InterArt Licensing

Golden August

Elisabeth Weaver Winstead

There are no words for saying
    How dazzling is the view
On golden days in August;
    The glowing sun beams true.

I love the month of August—
    Her gentle, peaceful breeze,
The bounty of rich farmlands,
    The brimming orchard trees.

The year now turns to August,
    A glim'ring gold array,
The golden month of sunshine
    When blooms add rich display.

Then August spreads the colors
    That linger in our eyes—
The bloom of golden poppies,
    Bright wings of butterflies.

The evening show'rs bring rainbows,
    Bright wonders to behold
Of coral, gold, and purple—
    A color-fest, so bold.

At night the moon's bright halo
    Shines down from the dark sky;
The golden starlight twinkles
    O'er Summer's last goodbye.

2

POPPIES
Antelope Valley, California
Ron Thomas/FPG International

A Loving Home

M. M. Marshall

A loving home is a lighthouse
With children safe and warm,
Refuge from the cold outside,
A port in time of storm,

A harbor for the family,
A haven in the night,
A beacon that burns brightly
To shed abroad its light.

When time has passed, the children leave
For shelters of their own.
May each be guided by the light
Of love in every home.

PORTLAND HEAD LIGHT
Portland, Maine
Fred M. Dole
New England Stock Photography

Plans

Helen Morgan Brooks

My sister and I
(We've said this before)
Will build a new house,
And she'll plan the door.

I know what she wants;
For I know her you see:
No fancy doodads
Or frail filigree,

A stout, oaken door,
Perhaps painted white,
A wrought iron knocker
With a chain for the night.

But me, now,
Without any talent or flair,
I'm equally determined
To work on the stair.

A gay, spiral stairway
I've planned so it seems,
With bottom steps wide
Where children have dreams;

Then midway between
The bottom and top,
A broad sort of landing
Where old folk may stop;

And brides, laughingly
Ascending this way,
May pause and look back
To toss their bouquet.

Tumble-down Cottage

Patience Strong

There's a tumble-down cottage
    in the shade of a tree
Off a little, green lane
    that runs down to the sea;
Just a crumbling, tumbling
    sort of affair,
A bit of a ruin,
    but what do I care?

Its casements look out
    to white dunes and blue seas
Flung wide to the sun
    and the fresh, salty breeze,
And only the cry
    of the gulls wheeling by
Breaks the sweet peace
    of the earth and the sky.

And when with the sunset
    the purple dusk falls,
A soft, rosy glow
    rests on windows and walls;
And on the quiet heart
    as the light fades away,
God's blessing descends
    at the close of the day.

A DAY AT THE SHORE
Original Painting by Linda Nelson Stocks

©Linda Nelson Stocks
1993

BITS & PIECES

Ride softly that you may get home the sooner.
English Proverb

For the only happy toilers under
Earth's majestic dome
Are the ones who find their glories
In the little spot called home.
Valli Rose

Go not abroad for happiness.
For see, it is a flower that blooms
at thy door. Bring love and justice home,
and then no more thou'lt wonder in
what dwelling joy may be.
Minot J. Savage

Home is a box of jewels, more precious
than diamonds or fine rubies. Here in childhood
dwelt your mother's love; here, in riper years,
the love of your children and their mother.
Albert B. Galloway

𝒜 house is built of logs and stone,
Of tiles and posts and piers;
A home is built of loving deeds
That stand a thousand years.
Victor Hugo

𝒮uch is the patriot's boast, where'er we roam,
His first, best country ever is at home.
Oliver Goldsmith

𝒪 fortunate, O happy day,
When a new household finds its place
Among the myriad homes of earth,
Like a new star just sprung to birth.
Henry Wadsworth Longfellow

ℋome—the place where our stomachs
get three square meals a day and our hearts
a thousand.
Charles M. Crowe

𝒫eace be within thy walls,
and prosperity within thy palaces.
Psalm 122:7

11

The Old Porch Swing

Ruth H. Underhill

Something I miss on a house today
Is the old porch swing where we would sway.
When we were kids we'd sit in a row
And gently rock it to and fro.

This was our seat on a rainy day;
We would sit and watch the raindrops play.
We'd listen to the loud thunder roar
And watch the lightning streak and soar.

And then upon a sunshine day,
We'd gather up our dolls to play.
And out they'd go to the old porch swing,
Our close haven from everything.

When baby brother would fret and cry,
Mother would rock him bye and bye.
His tiny head nestled near her chin;
She'd forward rock then back again.

It seems like such an age ago
When gently we'd rock to and fro.
And then a sweet melody we'd sing
And gently sway in the old porch swing.

HANDCRAFTED PORCH SWING WITH WOOD ACCENTS
James R. Levin/FPG International

Readers' Reflections

Editor's Note: Readers are invited to submit unpublished, original poetry for possible publication in future issues of Ideals. *Please send typed copies only; manuscripts will not be returned. Writers receive $10 for each published submission. Send material to* Readers' Reflections, Ideals Publications Inc., 535 Metroplex Drive, Suite 250, Nashville, Tennessee 37211.

My Stroll Down Memory Lane

At eventide I often dream;
   Thus in my thoughts I roam,
And so I stroll down mem'ry lane
   On paths that lead to home.

I see my father standing there
   Beside the hedgerow green;
The roses too are blossoming—
   Oh, what a lovely scene:

The kitchen with its spicy smells
   That I have known before,
And Mother with her apron on
   Stands by the old back door.

The hollyhocks and bleeding hearts,
   Lilacs, and trumpet vine
Help me recall a fragrance sweet
   Within this heart of mine.

I see the dolls all set in place,
   The table set for tea,
The old, brown bear sits on the bench—
   All waiting there for me.

No more am I a little girl;
   To womanhood I've grown.
And now I sit and ponder
   As to where the years have flown.

The walks my folks and I would take
   Down to old Robin Hill;
The wheel that e'er was turning
   By the stores at Splinterville;

The picnics there in summertime
   And boat rides on the lake;
To swim in the ol' swimmin' hole—
   Oh yes, what fun 'twould make.

I treasure so those yesteryears;
   They weave a tapestry,
A treasure chest of memories
   That mean the world to me.

So whenever I feel lonely
   And my heart yearns to roam,
I drift away in memory
   Down those paths that lead to home.

Mary E. Randall Herrington
Phoenix, Arizona

The Second Generation

I walk into my kitchen nook
    And take a quick and hurried look
To see it neat and sparkling clear
    And think of days of yesteryear

When dirty dishes piled high.
    You almost thought that they would fly!
The knives and forks were strewn about,
    Plus water dripping from the spout.

A hundred glasses lined the sink;
    Each one produced a thirsty drink.
The screen door (swung on one bent hinge)
    Would catch the curtain by the fringe.

But now the scene is still and mild.
    Gone are the voices shrill and wild.
But wait, what is that noise I hear?
    The grandkids have arrived, oh dear!

Theresa I. Miles
Gulfport, Mississippi

Just Deserts

(Dedicated to Joe Flaherty, Jr.)

There's a roaring in the kitchen;
    There's a grinding in the sink.
Our walls and floors are twitching,
    And I can scarcely think.

Pots and pans come tumbling
    Out the cupboard door;
Every chair goes rumbling
    'Cross the squeaky floor.

Lids and jars are battling;
    The radio pounds a beat;
Silverware is rattling,
    Creative license indeed!

I'm glad I'm not the cook,
    Being served is such a treat,
And I am grateful truly
    For this good food we eat.

But tonight the master chef presides
    Over boxes and tin cans,
And oh what cacophony abides
    In meals cooked by his hands!

Linda Marie Flaherty
Baltimore, Maryland

My World

No matter what the weather,
    Though it be cold or hot,
I never let it phase me;
    For I have found my spot

Where things are as I want them,
    Exactly right for me.
I never found the outside world
    To be my cup of tea.

Each room is as I've planned it,
    A portion of myself,
From pictures in the hallway
    To the books upon the shelf.

Each item that I gaze on
    Holds a memory all its own,
From the basketful of daisies
    To the rose that stands alone.

My life, my thoughts, my feelings
    Are captured in each room,
And that is why I feel secure
    As a moth in a cocoon.

Carol Neumann
Jersey City, New Jersey

THROUGH MY WINDOW

Art by Russ Flint

THE NEW AGE OF HOME ECONOMICS

Home economics has changed a lot since I was in school. The way I recall it, we girls all signed up for Home Ec, and the boys all signed up for Shop. We made biscuits, white sauce, and meatloaf and sewed "garments." The boys made cutting boards and step stools and sometimes book ends. Things were simple. Not so today. When my sons reached their teens, they couldn't wait to sign up for Home Ec.

"Why not Shop?" I asked.

"Mom," my oldest retorted, with that tone reserved for parents and other dull species, "nobody takes Shop. Home Ec is much cooler. Besides, you get to eat stuff in Home Ec."

Ah ha! Here was the secret behind how educators lured young men out of the garage and into the kitchen. Well, I certainly didn't want to stand in the way of modern education. Besides, it would be nice to have a man around the house who could fix something besides a fried-egg sandwich.

I waited what I considered a respectable length of time before inquiring about the progress of my newest home economist. I was hopeful he might volunteer to make dinner one night as extra credit.

"So, how's the Home Ec class going?" I asked.

"Oh, great. We're doing frogs," my son replied.

"Aren't frogs' legs a little advanced for a beginning cooking project?"

"Mom," there was that tone again, "we are definitely *not* eating frogs. We're sewing them and stuffing them with beans. They're great at the football games. Do you know how far up the grandstand you can toss a frog?"

I had to admit ignorance on that one. "Real far, I'll bet," was all I could respond. This was Home Ec? Where were the biscuits and meatloaf?

16

I decided it was best not to ask too many questions, but I kept looking for clues as to when the cooking unit was going to begin. I became hopeful during the second semester when my son asked me if he could have two eggs for school.

"Hard boiled or raw?" I asked and began to envision egg salad or some kind of sauce or dessert.

"Raw ones. I need two because I have to do twins," he responded.

"Twins? What kind of a dish is twins?" I asked.

"Oh, we're doing a unit on family living, and I have to carry around two raw eggs all week and take care of them like they were twins. This is supposed to get us to see how hard it is to take care of babies. I have to keep them with me all the time or else get a baby sitter for them if I have to go out or something. Neat, huh?"

"You aren't going to cook them?" I asked.

"Oh, no. I'd flunk for child abuse if I did that. Bye, Mom."

He tenderly wrapped each egg in a paper towel and tucked one in the toe of each gym shoe. He grinned at me as he held up the shoes and pronounced them "baby carriers!" Then he ducked out the door.

What had happened to Home Ec? My son was making beanbags and caring for egg babies, and I was getting no closer to my goal of a gourmet meal prepared by a male member of my family.

Near the end of the school year, I had a glimmer of hope. "We're doing cooking for the rest of the year, Mom. Ms. Clark says we're finally ready for the basic elements of all life: fire and water."

"You're going to boil water after all this time?" Well, it was a start. I had to admit, Ms. Clark certainly had a flair for the dramatic.

Weeks passed, and I heard nothing more about Home Ec until one day in late spring. My son jogged in the door after school and announced, "Don't plan anything for dinner tomorrow, Mom. I'm cooking. It's our final exam, and you all have to fill out an evaluation sheet on my meal. Can I have some money to go buy groceries?"

I handed over the money with some reservations. After all, this was a kid who sewed frogs and packed egg babies in his gym shoes.

The next night when we sat down to dinner, I gave the younger kids a whispered reminder to eat whatever their brother had fixed. My husband said the blessing as usual, but his tone was especially prayerful as he mentioned the food.

Our young chef disappeared into the kitchen then returned proudly bearing his creation: "Pasta salad with ham and broccoli, fresh fruit, and Armenian flatbread!" He set each dish down with a flourish and grinned at us with satisfaction.

"Wow," I managed. "This looks great!"

"And it's well-balanced too, Mom. You see, you have to have your food pyramid values, you know, grains and vegetables and proteins and stuff; and to get the most out of them, they shouldn't be overcooked. Did you know that broccoli is a proven anti-carcinogen?"

He shoved a mouthful of pasta into his mouth, and I nudged his father under the table before he could say anything in response.

"Is that so?" I said as I buttered a piece of flatbread.

"Watch those animal fats, Mom, they'll kill you." He waved his fork in the direction of my buttered bread.

"Other things could get you first!" my husband countered with just a bit of an edge to his voice.

We completed our dinner, and each family member dutifully filled out the evaluation. As my son collected them, he was riding high on the tide of his culinary success. "Well, I guess I'll just go write my wrap-up," he announced.

"Not quite yet," I suggested. "Did Ms. Clark tell you about the other basic elements of life?" He looked puzzled. "Detergent and elbow grease," I said as I directed his attention to the dirty dishes and cluttered kitchen.

"Oh, Mom, come on! I've been in the kitchen all afternoon!"

I smiled and handed him a sponge. "In the great pyramid of life, my dear, cleaning up is the cornerstone. Besides," I added with a poke in his ribs, "washing dishes is a proven anti-carcinogen!"

Pamela Kennedy is a freelance writer of short stories, articles, essays, and children's books. Wife of a naval officer and mother of three children, she has made her home on both U.S. coasts and currently resides in Honolulu, Hawaii. She draws her material from her own experiences and memories, adding highlights from her imagination to enhance the story.

Dust Bunnies

Darlene Christianson

Weapons in hand, I grit my teeth
And face the challenge I must.
With mops and brooms and rubber gloves,
I prepare to battle The Dust.

I shoo the bunnies from under the bed;
They tumble across the room.
I hunt them down with vigilant eye
Then swat them with my broom.

I scrunch down on the floor to choose
A dustball specimen.
I lift a few straws for a peek
Then WHOOSH! They're off again

Around the room and through the door
And down the stairs and back.
I stay in hot pursuit; I'm not
Your average cleaning hack!

They leave a trail of filthy dust;
I spot them from the hall.
There's no escape for bunnies now;
They're bunched up by the wall.

Trapped at last, you fuzzy balls;
This time I've really won!
I raise my broom in victory—
Back under the bed they run.

COUNTRY BEDROOM
Jessie Walker Associates

One of These Days

Helena Ramage

One of these days
I'll become house-proud.
All my windows will gleam
As sunbeams shine through them.
The kitchen floor will be spotless—
Mopped every morning, waxed each week.
Rugs vacuumed, parlor furniture dutifully
Polished with delightfully smelly lemon oil.
My wash will flap on the line each day,
The bed sheets waving in the breeze.
I'll have my closets in perfect order—
A place for everything,
Everything in its place!
No dripping faucets or heating problems
To vex me.
Leftovers in the fridge will emerge
As mouth-watering casseroles!
Anyone entering my house
Will savor the fragrance
Of fresh-baked bread and cookies for tea.

Meanwhile, there are stories to tell,
A kitten to stroke,
Flowers to gather,
A shady bench under the oak tree—
A place to read and dream.

The world outside my house
Beckons me.
So I sigh and close the door behind me,
And I think about one of these days
When I will do something
About my untidy house.

Ideals' Family Recipes

Favorite Recipes from the Ideals Family of Readers

Editor's Note: Please send us your best-loved recipes! Mail a typed copy of the recipe along with your name, address, and telephone number to Ideals magazine, ATTN: Recipes, 535 Metroplex Drive, Suite 250, Nashville, Tennessee 37211. We will pay $10 for each recipe used. Recipes cannot be returned.

BUTTERSCOTCH COOKIES

Preheat oven to 350° F. In a large bowl, combine ½ cup butter, ½ cup firmly packed brown sugar, and 1 egg; mix until light. Add 1 teaspoon vanilla; mix well.

In a small bowl, sift together 1½ cups flour, ½ teaspoon baking soda, ½ teaspoon cream of tartar, and ¼ teaspoon salt; add to creamed mixture; mix well. Stir in one 3½-ounce package instant butterscotch pudding mix and ½ cup quick-cooking rolled oats; mix well.

Roll into small balls (½ inch diameter) and place 1 inch apart on an ungreased cookie sheet. Flatten with the bottom of a drinking glass. Bake 10 minutes or until edges are golden.

Mary Ellen Thieman
Cross Plains, Indiana

NO-BAKE COOKIES

In a medium saucepan, combine 2 cups granulated sugar, 3 tablespoons cocoa, ½ cup milk, and ½ cup butter; place over medium heat and bring to a rolling boil. Boil for 1 minute, then remove from heat. Add ½ teaspoon vanilla, ½ cup peanut butter, and 3 cups quick-cooking oats; mix well. Drop the dough by spoonfuls onto waxed paper. Let cookies cool until firm.

Betty Jo Stewart
Crawford, Colorado

LEMON DOODLES

Preheat oven to 400° F. In a large mixing bowl, combine 1 cup softened shortening, 1½ cups granulated sugar, 2 eggs, and 1½ teaspoons lemon extract; cream until light. In a separate mixing bowl, sift together 3 cups flour, 2 teaspoons cream of tartar, 1 teaspoon baking soda, and ¼ teaspoon salt. Stir dry mixture into creamed mixture; mix well. Chill dough in refrigerator at least 1 hour. Roll into 1-inch balls. Roll balls in granulated sugar and place 2 inches apart on an ungreased cookie sheet. Bake 8 minutes or until lightly browned.

Betty S. Young
Sewickley, Pennsylvania

THIMBLE COOKIES

Preheat oven to 325° F. In a large mixing bowl, combine ½ cup butter or margarine and ⅓ cup granulated sugar; cream until light. Reserving the egg white, add 1 egg yolk; beat well. Add 1 cup flour and 1 teaspoon vanilla; beat well. Roll batter into small balls about 1-inch in diameter. Dip each cookie in unbeaten egg white and then roll in 1 cup crushed walnuts. Bake on an ungreased cookie sheet 15 to 20 minutes. Remove from oven. Immediately press a hole in the center of each cookie with the end of a thimble. Remove from cookie sheet. When cool, fill the hole in each cookie with jelly. Makes 2 dozen.

Hilda Swanson
Minneapolis, Minnesota

PINWHEELS

In a large mixing bowl, combine ¾ cup butter or margarine and 1 cup granulated sugar; cream until fluffy. Add 2 eggs and 1 teaspoon vanilla; beat well. Set aside.

In a medium mixing bowl, combine 2½ cups flour, 1 teaspoon baking powder, and 1 teaspoon salt. Gradually add dry ingredients to creamed mixture; blend well. Divide dough in half.

In a small saucepan, heat over low heat 2 one-ounce squares of unsweetened baking chocolate until melted. Remove from heat and let cool. Add cooled chocolate to half of the cookie dough; blend well. Cover and refrigerate both halves of dough until firm.

Preheat oven to 400° F. Roll each half of dough into a 12-x-9-inch rectangle. Brush chocolate layer with warm milk; place plain layer atop the chocolate layer. Roll up jelly-roll fashion from long side. Wrap in plastic wrap and chill until firm. Cut the roll into ¼-inch slices. Place the slices on an ungreased cookie sheet and bake 8 to 10 minutes or until set. Remove from cookie sheet to a wire rack to cool. Makes about 4 or 5 dozen.

Allison Worthen
Turlock, California

My Favorite Recipe

June Masters Bacher

A handful of dewdrops
Dissolved in fresh air,
A slice of bright sunshine
Leavened in prayer,

All blended together
With neighbor and kin,
A dash of gay laughter
With love sifted in!

"Oh, to have a little house!
To own the hearth
and stool and all!"

—*Padraic Colum*

Handmade Heirloom

Mary Skarmeas

BREAD DOUGH CRAFTS

read has been called the staff of life throughout the ages for its ability to comfort and nourish us. Yet basic bread dough can provide more than simple sustenance. It can be used for a rewarding keepsake craft that the whole family will enjoy.

Creative dough art is a craft that flourishes with the imagination of the craftsperson; it is the type of craft that takes on the personality of the one whose hands are shaping the dough. Whether you use cut-out shapes or hand-molded figures, unique treasures can result. These treasures can be preserved as lasting heirlooms with a couple of coats of shellac or polyurethane.

Although dough crafts were originally made from a true unleavened bread dough, they are now often created from a variety of ingredients. The basic ingredients of most dough crafts are flour, salt, and water; but other ingredients can also make a suitable and interesting alternative. Dough made from applesauce and ground cinnamon, for example, has a wonderful aroma and color. Adding food coloring or dry cocoa to the basic dough will give a soft tint to the finished piece.

Using dough for purposes other than food consumption is an old endeavor. Ancient civilizations have left evidence of dough figures that were used by Greeks, Romans, and Egyptians to pay homage to their gods. In nineteenth-century Germany, where Christmas trees gained popularity, tree ornaments were crafted out of dough and hung with ribbons on the scented branches. To discourage hungry field mice from devouring the ornaments, the Germans began adding a lot of salt to the dough; their idea led to the term *salt dough*, which is often used to refer to bread dough crafts.

Immigrants to the New World brought the knowledge of bread dough crafts with them. During the first half of this century, the art of decorating dough was lost due to the scarcity of salt during World War I. It remained forgotten until the 1960s when interest in folk art experienced a resurgence, and dough art was rediscovered. More recently, dough art can be seen in many types of crafts and even the reproduction of food products such as shellacked bread and bagels. All types of little objects have appeared—charms, lapel pins, knickknacks, and even magnets—that have an enchanting appeal for all. Today's dough art often includes decorative touches such as paint, cake decorations, or even dried flowers.

Using a basic recipe of four cups all-purpose flour, one cup salt, and enough water to form a smooth dough, a variety of charming objects can be created. One project that caught my eye was a wreath made from dough tinted light brown with cocoa. The project would provide many hours of absorbing fun for children as well as adults. The wreath has leaves that are easily cut from rolled-out dough. The leaves are then placed on a ring of dough that is about six inches in diameter and one half-inch thick and set on a piece of aluminum foil. Make fruit of a size to fit on the leaves and add tiny, nut-shaped balls. To add

color, work food coloring into the dough or paint the wreath with watercolors after baking. Bake the wreath on foil in a 170° F oven one hour for every quarter-inch thickness of the dough. In other words, a wreath with the thickest point measuring one and one-half inches would require six hours of baking at 170° F. After this initial baking time, increase the temperature to 200° F and bake for another half-hour. Finally, increase the temperature to 250° F and bake for one more half-hour. Allow to cool, then peel back the foil. Several coats of thick shellac, with adequate drying times between coats, will add luster and preserve these lovely wreaths.

A completely different but equally interesting dough recipe is made from warm applesauce and ground cinnamon. To form a pliable dough, combine about one and a half times as much cinnamon as applesauce. The project requires a lot of cinnamon, but the result is a dough the color of earthenware pottery that has a wonderfully spicy aroma (if shellac is not used).

It is always a pleasure to create something out of ordinary, everyday ingredients. It is also fun to find an activity that we can share with family or friends as well as enjoy alone. Even the smallest child loves to play with dough. While the little ones are playing, ask them to imprint their hands on a flat round of dough. After baking and cooling these small plaques, add each child's name and the date with watercolors. An afternoon craft will quickly become a precious keepsake that will bring back heartwarming memories in the years to come.

Creating an heirloom doesn't have to be an expensive, highly skilled production. A cherished heirloom can come from something as basic as bread dough as long as it is made with a love that is passed down through generations.

"Comfort thine heart with a morsel of bread."

Judges 19:5

Mary Skarmeas lives in Danvers, Massachusetts, and is studying for her bachelor's degree in English at Suffolk University. Mother of four and grandmother of one, Mary loves all crafts, especially knitting.

Silken Beams, Silver Dreams

Donna Stringfellow

A mid-air contractor moves unafraid.
On high-rise silk beams, she plies her trade,
Edging along on the silvery tier,
Constructing each crossbeam, girder, and pier.

Her aerial work seems done with ease
On near-hidden sites among the trees.
Balancing tiptoe above the ground,
She stretches new wires both upward and down.

The supports are all set; she stables the sides
Then shores up the mean so nothing divides.
She is just like a smart architect,
Designing a new masterpiece to erect.

A true engineer with heart and soul,
She needs no blueprint to be told
That the best way to keep the tum fed
Is simply to build an e'er-stronger web.

COLLECTOR'S CORNER

Lisa C. Thompson

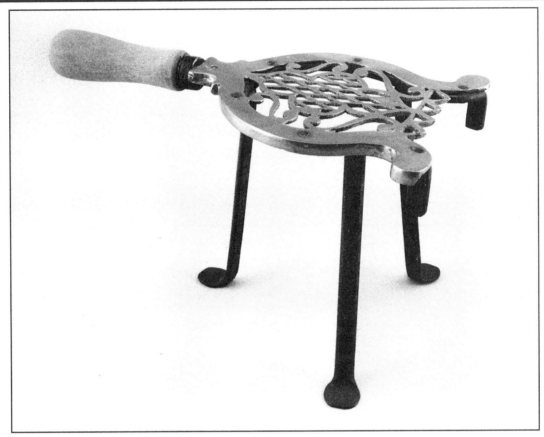

BRASS AND IRON HEARTH TRIVET WITH LYRE-SHAPED TOP. Shelburne Museum, Shelburne, Vermont.

TRIVETS

The heart of the home lies in the kitchen, and the kitchen has always been a good source for collectibles—from cookbooks and Fiesta dinnerware to spoons and butter molds. Trivets are another collectible that bring to mind the warmth of the hearth and the comfort of home.

The word trivet comes from the Latin word *tripes*, which means three-footed. There are three types of trivets; all of which are worthy of collecting: tabletop trivets used to protect surfaces from hot dishes, long-legged trivets used to keep dishes warm on the open hearth, and spade-shaped trivets used to hold antique flatirons. The tabletop

variety were formed from many different materials, including brass, copper, nickel-plate, sterling silver, wire, cut-glass, pottery, tile, and china. Flatiron trivets and hearth trivets were always made of hand-wrought iron or, in later years, cast iron.

Trivets have been used in America since the first pilgrims journeyed to the New World in the wake of the *Niña*, the *Pinta*, and the *Santa Maria*. These early trivets were constructed of hand-wrought iron and sported three long legs. They held large, simmering pots or kettles over the cooking fire. Three legs were used instead of four because the three-legged trivet was easier to level on the uneven floor of the fireplace. Trivets remained a necessary part of the American household until the early 1900s when iron wood-burning stoves for cooking began to replace open hearths in the kitchen. Flatiron trivets declined in use at about the same time due to the introduction of the electric iron in 1882.

Throughout the 1700s and early 1800s in America, trivets were painstakingly shaped by hand out of iron by the village blacksmith. These early, hand-wrought trivets are treasured today by collectors and are therefore more valuable than modern reproductions. Crude in comparison to the fancier cast-iron trivets, the hand-hammered styles were simple, with circles, squares, and triangles predominating and few detailed designs. Early tabletop and flatiron trivets often included wooden handles.

Every foundry in America was mass producing cast trivets by the mid-1800s, with cast-iron being the most popular medium. New designs and motifs flooded the market. The most popular included eagles, rosettes, lovebirds, roosters, and lacy or geometric patterns. The trivets often bore the mark of the foundry that produced them, but many sported trade names, mottoes, dates, and insignias. Manufacturers began to commission trivets bearing their company's logo to hand out as advertising. Stoveworks were one of the biggest producers of trivets, which were designed to complement the maker's stoves and often passed out to potential buyers to promote the product.

Miniature trivets, some as small as two-and-a-quarter inches, were initially designed as samples but later became popular as toys to hold toy flatirons. These miniature models were created in practically as many designs as the full-scale trivets.

ANTIQUE CAST-IRON TRIVETS.
Shelburne Museum, Shelburne, Vermont.

During the Victorian era, the ritual of afternoon tea encouraged the development of brass trivets that were designed to hook over the edge of a brass fireplace fender and warm the teakettle. Also called footmen, these brass trivets were typically highly ornate in keeping with the Victorian style. In addition, many of the pottery and china trivets from the Victorian era were used under teapots in the parlor.

Authentic antique trivets are often difficult to distinguish from reproductions. During the 1960s, iron reproductions were made in mass quantities in Europe and Japan. These copies sold well in the American market and fooled even the savviest collectors. The early trivets are usually thinner and stronger than their modern counterparts because the early models were cast in a fine sand and used a different quality of iron. The impostors have a thicker frame and usually look too perfect; antique trivets often have an uneven top, due to years of use, and an unpolished underside. Another clue that a trivet is authentic is an imperfection or two from an excess of molten iron beyond the mold. Rust, however, is not necessarily a clue to authenticity. Disreputable dealers can rust a new trivet easily by immersing it in water. The best way to determine whether or not a trivet is truly made of iron is with a magnet. Copper and brass naturally repel magnets.

A collection of antique trivets in a kitchen adds a nostalgic touch reminiscent of yesteryear. The masterful American craftsmen who designed and shaped these humble utensils used a flourish of detail and style equal to that of the finest artisans. It is this unique heritage that makes trivets such a popular collectible with those who appreciate the fine craftsmanship, warm nostalgia, and artistic heritage of our country.

Unimportant Things

Mamie Ozburn Odum

I love unimportant things—
Fluffy down on birdies' wings;
Sunlight, stars, and dancing leaves;
Tiny hands in outing sleeves;
Rosy glow at dawn of day;
Squirrels busy at their play;
Happy smiles of friends I've met;
Changing hues when sun has set;
Shadow soft on rose-hung laths;
Tiny, winding meadow paths;
Softened notes of night bird's cry;
Dear old song, "Sweet Bye and Bye";
Father's love and Mother's kiss—
My heart yearns for things like this.

A Thing of Beauty

John Keats

A thing of beauty is a joy forever;
Its loveliness increases. It will never
Pass into nothingness; but still will keep
A bower quiet for us, and a sleep
Full of sweet dreams, and health, and quiet breathing.

Yes, in spite of all,
Some shape of beauty moves away the pall
From our dark spirits. Such the sun, the moon,
Trees old, and young, sprouting a shady boon
For simple sheep; and such are daffodils
With the green world they live in; and clear rill
That for themselves a cooling covert make
'Gainst the hot season; the mid forest brake,
Rich with a sprinkling of fair musk rose blooms
And such too is the grandeur of the dooms
We have imagined for the mighty dead;
All lovely tales that we have heard or read:
An endless fountain of immortal drink,
Pouring unto us from the heaven's brink.

BICYCLE AND FLOWER BASKET
Hailey, Idaho
Michael Olenick
F-Stock

LEGENDARY AMERICANS

NANCY SKARMEAS

ELLEN HENRIETTA SWALLOW RICHARDS

Chemistry and homemaking. At first glance they appear to have little in common, but it is in the common ground between these two fields that Ellen Henrietta Swallow Richards found her calling. In so doing, she improved life for American women and American families.

Born in Dunstable, Massachusetts, in 1842, Ellen Swallow received her early education at home from her parents and later attended college at Vassar, where she discovered her passion for the sciences, particularly chemistry and astronomy. After Vassar, Swallow was accepted as the first female student at the Massachusetts Institute of Technology (MIT); in 1873, she became the first woman to earn a degree at the prestigious school. Swallow faced great barriers of discrimination during her years at MIT. She was admitted as a special student in chemistry and awarded what she was told was a full scholarship; in truth, she attended free of charge because the school's trustees were unwilling to officially accept a woman student. Swallow kept a low profile at MIT, aware that her status was always in question by some and that her opportunity to further her studies was dependent upon the good will of college officials. She pursued graduate study after earning her bachelor's degree but found that the path to a doctorate was not open to female students.

Because of her own struggles against discrimination, Richards wanted to smooth the path for women who would follow. After her marriage to mining and metallurgical engineering professor Robert Richards, she made the decision to combine her interest in chemistry with the need to improve educational opportunities for women in the sciences. Richards established a Woman's Laboratory at MIT and also organized a science section in the Society to Encourage Studies at Home, a correspondence school for women.

Richards's efforts to recruit more women into science training at MIT confirmed to her the serious barriers to higher education faced by so many American women of her day—so bogged down were they in domestic chores and so often troubled were they by persistent poor health that they had little time and little inclination to pursue interests outside the home, much less to take on scientific study. Richards, who had been raised by parents with a keen interest in bringing simplicity and efficiency to their household chores, began to devote her energies to teaching women about good health, proper nutrition, and efficient cleaning and housekeeping.

Richards was not a radical by any means. She did not advocate that women free themselves from domestic chores but rather free themselves from the unnecessary drudgery of domestic work. By helping women learn how to make their homes more comfortable and more efficient, and themselves more healthy and energetic, Richards hoped to free their time and their energies for academic pursuits. Her own home was a showcase of her ideas. Heavy draperies were replaced by light, easy-to-clean curtains; carpets were removed in favor of hardwood floors. She had a vacuum cleaner, a gas range, a shower, and a telephone—modern conveniences that helped to simplify household work.

In time, Richards developed a new field of study—home economics. The term itself originated at a series of summer conferences Richards organized in Lake Placid, New York, in the 1890s. Attending these conferences were individuals committed to the common cause of the "betterment of the American home." In 1908, Richards became president of a new organization called the American Home Economic Association, which was based upon the principles of the Lake Placid Conferences. The Association was dedicated to the "improvement of living conditions in the home, the institutional household, and the community." Eventually, Richards was named supervisor of the teaching of home economics by the National Education Association. Her vision of women free from drudgery and in good physical health, running clean and efficient homes with time and energy left over for academic pursuits thus

began to make its way into the curriculum of American public schools; the home economics course was born.

Richards's interest covered the whole gamut of what we know as home economics. She emphasized good nutrition and proper food preparation. She stressed the importance of physical exercise for women. She researched efficient cleaning methods and studied household water supplies for impurities. She brought attention to some potential poisons in household products; and with students at the Woman's Laboratory at MIT, she conducted experiments on common food additives and cleaning materials.

Richards understood that as Americans moved in ever-increasing numbers to the city, they lost touch with the way of life of the farm, a way of life in which every child learned the basics of household work from parents who were at home with the family during the day. Richards saw the family home as the center of American society. She believed that with families living in cities and parents working all day outside the home, it fell to the public schools to teach children the skills they needed to manage their homes and to live well.

Ellen Swallow Richards was a woman of boundless energy, unfailing generosity, and constant curiosity about every aspect of the world around her. She and her husband never had children of their own; but they opened their home to their students, thereby teaching good living by their own example. Richards was one of the true pioneers in scientific education for women and an early advocate of a cause still in need of support today. Thanks to her work, colleges and universities across the United States began to open their doors to bright, young women eager for careers in the sciences. Richards was, as she liked to say, the "engineer" of the field of home economics. By using the best principles of her scientific training, Swallows simplified household work; her years of dedication dignified domestic work by acknowledging its central value to American life.

The Way Things Are

Craig E. Sathoff

Though other homes are finer far,
I'm satisfied the way things are;
For in our little cottage small,
A blessed peace lies over all.
My precious jewels in bright array
Are three small children as they play.
No richer treasures can there be
Than healthy youngsters filled with glee.

I do not wish on lucky stars.
I'm satisfied the way things are.
My life is filled with lovely flowers—
The friends who share my free-time hours,
The neighbors who stop by to see
If I have time to sit for tea,
The joyful days of family fun,
The hearthside when my work is done.

I do not care to journey far.
I'm satisfied the way things are;
For home is where my interests lie,
The sparkling star that fills my sky.
My church, my friends, my family
Are things that mean the most to me.
The rarest gems just could not please
When paired with treasures such as these.

SUMMER HAVEN
Old Sturbridge Village, Massachusetts
Dick Dietrich Photography

A SLICE OF LIFE

Edgar A. Guest

THE GAIN

When life was bright and cheerful, he went singing on his way.
    He scarcely knew his neighbors or what sort of folks were they.
But he woke one dismal morning to find all his money gone,
    And he found that fame and fortune were not safe to lean upon.

The other day I met him, and he said, "It's very queer,
    But the fact is I am happier than I've been for many a year.
I've discovered friendly people living just across the street;
    I've discovered books and blossoms and the grass beneath my feet.

"Since the bank account has dwindled, I've discovered at my door
    A variety of blessings which I'd never known before.
I've discovered chess and checkers are not games which children play
    But are glorious entertainment when at home you choose to stay.

"Oh, we're richer now in spirit than we ever thought we'd be;
    There's a bond of true devotion binding all the family.
We have gained in faith and wisdom and in fellowship with flowers.
    And whatever loss may follow, these shall evermore be ours."

Edgar A. Guest began his illustrious career in 1895 at the age of fourteen when his work first appeared in the Detroit Free Press. *His column was syndicated in over 300 newspapers, and he became known as "The Poet of the People."*

Candles of Contentment

John C. Bonser

A little house, adorned with love,
Where candles of contentment glow
Holds pleasures that the very rich
Are seldom privileged to know.

A little house, whose roof protects
The happy dreams of childhood,
Is built on sturdy beams of faith
As well as on its floors of wood.

A humble home where those within
Are not too proud to kneel and pray
Contains a peace that overcomes
The hectic moments of each day.

A cottage where pink roses climb
Up trellises outside its walls

Displays a beauty rivaling
Bouquets arrayed in marble halls.

A little house whose memories
Stay sunshine bright in every room
Keeps out the storms of wind and rain
And sweeps away cobwebs of gloom.

How welcoming, as twilight falls,
The path up to that cottage door
Where dear hearts wait the safe return
Of loved ones coming home once more.

Till we ascend to mansions high
(That Someone paid for long ago),
Give thanks for each small house below
Where candles of contentment glow.

TRAVELER'S Diary

Heather McArthur

MOUNT VERNON. Back of estate facing Potomac River. Photograph courtesy of Virginia Division of Tourism.

MOUNT VERNON
Fairfax County, Virginia

In a 1793 letter to an English correspondent, George Washington wrote, "No estate in United America is more pleasantly situated." The father of our country was speaking of Mount Vernon, his home from 1754 until his death in 1799, which remains today as an enduring symbol of our American heritage.

Mount Vernon is indeed pleasantly situated, for it stands on a tree-crowned hilltop overlooking the wooded shores of the Potomac River. Only sixteen miles from Washington, D.C., Mount Vernon's location enabled Washington to commute by land

or water to the Federal city, Alexandria.

As a child, Washington lived with his family at Mount Vernon from 1735 until 1739. Later, in 1754, he acquired the estate by lease from his brother Lawrence's widow. He officially inherited the home and property in 1761. Although frequently called away from his home for military and political service, the years Washington spent at Mount Vernon with his wife Martha were his most peaceful.

During the forty-five years that Washington oversaw the estate, it expanded from 2,126 acres to nearly eight thousand. Traditional crops were cultivated on the grounds, including tobacco, corn, and wheat. The house itself was redesigned under the direction of Washington, who found the original farmhouse too small. Twenty-five years of additions and restorations to the earlier homestead culminated in the Mount Vernon that we know today. It is said that Washington himself designed the two-story outdoor living area that overlooks the peaceful Potomac.

Other remarkable features of the majestic estate include the expansive, two-story dining room that took twelve years to complete. It was in this dining room that Washington and French generals met to organize the impending Battle of Yorktown. It was also where Washington was notified of his presidency and where his body remained for three days before his burial.

Architectural details and distinct antiques fill the preserved rooms of Mount Vernon. Visitors to the home will notice the hand-carved, stucco ceilings that depict an agricultural theme. Rare antiques include the bed on which Washington died and the famous mahogany tambour secretary in his study. Also on display are Martha's jewels, including a dazzling flower-shaped diamond ring and a garnet necklace.

After Washington's death in 1799, the estate was passed to his nephew, Bushrod Washington. The subsequent owners of Mount Vernon failed to maintain its agricultural productivity, and the home began to suffer from an increasing number of unrestricted tourists.

Miss Ann Pamela Cunningham of South Carolina became aware of the potential threat to Mount Vernon and in 1853 founded the Mount Vernon Ladies' Association of the Union to save the historic home from ruin. This association was both the first national historic preservation organization and the first women's patriotic society in America. Through the many efforts of the Ladies' Association, Mount Vernon has been thoroughly restored to its appearance almost two hundred years ago when Washington graced its halls. Restoration projects continue year round.

Because of the meticulous care the estate has received, Mount Vernon is perhaps the best surviving example of social and economic plantation life in the South during the eighteenth century. Visitors may stroll through the thirty acres of beautiful gardens and wooded grounds, explore the various outbuildings where everyday activities such as bread baking and cloth weaving took place, and tour the plantation home itself. Also on the site are the tombs of George and Martha Washington as well as burial grounds of the many workers whose labor helped to make Mount Vernon a productive plantation.

More than fifty million people have visited Mount Vernon since the Ladies' Association first assumed control, and it remains one of our country's oldest ongoing preservation projects. With its centuries of American history and collection of personal artifacts, Mount Vernon offers an enlightening look at one of our country's most famous homes and its distinct heritage.

MOUNT VERNON INTERIORS. Fairfax County, Virginia.
Photographs courtesy of Virginia Division of Tourism.

Grandmother's Desk

Virginia Covington

The desk at which I sit to write
    Was Nana's long ago.
My heart was set upon it then;
    It's cherished now more so.

Her legacy is brought to me
    In cubbyholes and drawers,
And I now sit to send out love
    Where she did years before.

How warm it felt when Nana wrote
    A word, a wish, a cheer.
So now I want to do the same
    For those whom I hold dear.

Some paper, pens, and stamps are stashed
    In drawers and tiny slots.
The old desk beckons me, like her,
    To sit and gather thoughts.

Above the rich mahogany
    Rise shelves behind smooth glass.
From where I sit I gaze upon
    The books and photographs.

And there the kin of old and new
    By whom we've both been blessed
Are looking down upon the one
    Who's writing at the desk.

Family Reunion

Reginald Holmes

It's family reunion time
    And folks from miles away
Will meet again to celebrate
    Their very special day.
It's now the time for shaking hands,
    For smiles and also tears,
When folks are meeting relatives
    They haven't seen for years.

There's Auntie Bea and Cousin Sue
    And Walter, John, and Will;
There's Cousin Janie and boyfriend,
    And there comes Uncle Phil.
There are lots of lovely nieces
    With nephews by the score,
And at least a dozen babies
    We haven't seen before.

It's when old folks get together
    Away from toil and care,
And the youngsters are discussing
    The hopes and dreams they share.
It's the day when troubles vanish,
    A time to laugh and sing
While the ladies load the tables
    With food fit for a king.

There is ham and mashed potatoes,
    Baked beans, and apple pie;
Spice cake and fluffy biscuits,
    So tempting to the eye.
Then comes the time for parting;
    We wend our homeward way;
But what could be more wonderful
    Than our reunion day?

Keyed Up

June Wilcoxon Brown

There are various kinds of keys—Key West, keyboards, keystones, keynotes, Francis Scott Key. I have no problem with these keys. My antagonist is any key that unlocks a house or car door, safe or suitcase. I am a loser of keys.

For more years than I care to acknowledge, I have been a "Jenny" Appleseed of sorts by sowing keys from one end of the United States to the other and on several foreign shores. My sowing hasn't produced plump, red apples, just plump, red faces. These flushed faces appear on the unsuspecting individuals who happen to find my lost keys. They puzzle over what the keys might unlock, and then they unsuccessfully jab the mysterious keys into random locks. Nothing is more frustrating than an orphan key without a mother lock.

Losing keys is not my shortcoming alone. Friends are also afflicted, and we gravitate to each other like ants to a watermelon at a picnic. One friend solved her key-losing problem by buying a suitcase with a combination lock. Guess what? On her third trip with the suitcase, she forgot the combination. To get the correct numbers, she had to phone her ever-suffering husband long distance across the continent before she could floss her teeth and wiggle into her nightie.

Another friend blames his key-losing affliction for altering his education. As a first-year student at Harvard Law School, he waited in a Cambridge study room for a week while anticipating the delivery of the trunk that contained all his worldly goods. By the time it arrived, he had, of course, lost its key. When the locksmith unlocked it, the young man said, "If only everyone in this world were honest, we wouldn't even need keys." The locksmith nodded and added quickly, "Or lawyers either." My friend names this incident as the sole reason why he remained at Harvard Law School only long enough to discover the Boston Symphony Orchestra.

Garage keys, locker keys, office keys—give me any key, and I'll lose it. Though I don't ordinarily lose pins, I lost my college sorority pin. It was shaped like a key.

Egyptians started this key problem when they conceived the pin-tumbler lock, the forerunner of today's lock. Perhaps Cleopatra was the first Egyptian to lose a key. Give or take a year or two, five thousand years passed before American locksmith Linus Yale, Jr., in 1861, improved the Egyptian lock and created our modern one; thus began the Age of Key Losers.

The time lock, which was first used successfully in 1875, could be a godsend to key-losers if the time mechanism didn't need to

48

be set in advance. Waiting outside a burglar-proof door for a time lock to let you in while frozen food drips all over your linen dress isn't one of life's finer moments.

Combination locks were invented in the seventeenth century, probably by a key loser. Attached to my suitcase zippers, these locks suit me well because there are no keys for me to lose. (I stick adhesive tape bearing the secret numbers on the insides of my wrists.) I only wish combination locks fit doors.

Modern inventors made keys utilitarian. Up until the nineteenth century, keys resembled ornate, oversized "keys to cities" and were therefore harder to lose. One such key I didn't lose opened the door to our room in Mexico City's Genevé Hotel. Lamb-chop sized and attached to an identifying brass ping-pong paddle, the key, when dropped, sounded like a spilled pile of cake pans. The Genevé had given thought to key-losers. I didn't lose the key to our hotel room in Fajardo, Puerto Rico, either. There were no keys. If only it were always that easy.

Ancient Etruscans had keys. Their superiority and wealth were based on their knowledge of ironworking. One might say their ironwork was the "key" to their success. The coat-of-arms of the Holy See bears two crossed keys. I should use crossed keys in my own personal coat-of-arms in recognition of how "cross" lost keys make me.

In religion and art, the key often symbolizes authority. For me, keys symbolize frantic hours searching through purses and drawers, peering under couches and pillows, and hunting the floors of sundry department stores, supermarkets, and post offices.

Although I can never find the key I need, I can always find other mysterious keys. Since I never remember what doors the numerous keys tucked here and there around the house open, I commandeered an old jewelry box as a treasure chest for mongrel keys (even though I didn't know what they were treasured for). Sometimes we resort to this box when I've lost a key to something. Something like the closet (at such inopportune times as when my precious, and usually brilliant, grandson has managed somehow to lock himself in).

But none of these keys fits any of our locks. Still, I am a coward. I haven't the courage or strength of character to close my eyes and drop the stray keys in the trash. If I did, my husband would immediately ask, "Where is the key to that old buffalo duffel bag I gave you twenty years ago?" If I couldn't produce it in five seconds, he would shake his head and say *again*, "I can't understand why you're always losing keys."

In desperation, my husband, who can tell you where his first grade locker key is, finally hit upon a scheme to reduce the mortality rate of my keys. He placed a covered cloisonné bonbon dish on the table in the entrance hall. Every time (well, most of the time) I enter the front door, my keys go there, unless I have lost any keys between the garage and the house.

I'll admit, the new method doesn't work all the time; but my husband knows I'm "trying" (in more ways than one), so he's not so "keyed-up" these days. Now, if you will please excuse me, I must go out to the backyard to search for the key to the basement door.

FOR THE CHILDREN

ARTWORK BY RUSS FLINT

DOORBELLS
Rachel Field

You never know with a doorbell
    Who may be ringing it—
It may be Great-aunt Cynthia
    To spend the day and knit;
It may be a peddler with things to sell
    (I'll buy some when I'm older);
Or the grocer's boy with his apron on
    And a basket on his shoulder;
It may be the old umbrella-man
    Giving his queer, cracked call;
Or a lady dressed in rustly silk,
    With card-case and parasol.
Doorbells are like a magic game
    Or the grab bag at a fair—
You never know when you hear one ring
    Who may be waiting there!

The unique perspective of Russ Flint's artistic style has made him a favorite of Ideals *readers for many years. A resident of California and father of four, Russ Flint has illustrated a children's Bible and many other books.*

Trolley Ride

Ray I. Hoppman

Remember the old open trolley
That ran back in years rather far
When chartered by groups for a journey
With cross seats the width of the car?

The ladies provided the lunches
To picnic that beautiful day.
The chaperone, Aunt Anybody,
E'er knew what to do and to say.

The girls in their mutton sleeve blouses
With little, stuffed birds on their hats,
The men with their banded straw skimmers
And stickpins in gaudy cravats,

They sang the old songs "In the Gloaming,"
"Ben Bolt," and the hit "Dolly Gray"
And danced in the spacious pavilion
Until came the sunset of day.

Then boarding the car for returning,
A little bit spent, every one,
To sing "Home, Sweet Home" was tradition.
Oh, trolley rides surely were fun!

TONSORIAL PARLOR Lee Dubin, Artist
Courtesy of the Artist and Wild Wings, Inc.
Lake City, Minnesota

Scissors, Comb, and Shears

Jon N. McCready

I lost some hair the other day.
It disappeared the same old way;
A man I've known for fifty years
Applied his scissors, comb, and shears.

We met when I was but a lad,
An introduction from my dad.
I greeted him with childish tears,
The man with scissors, comb, and shears.

'Bout once a month on Saturday
It got to where I'd hear him say,
"It must be time to lower ears
And use the scissors, comb, and shears."

Through junior high my hair was short
While playing on the hardwood court.
He came to see most all our games
And even knew the players' names.

A jolly man, he seemed to know
That hair styles change as young men grow.
To be accepted by my peers,
The hair soon covered both my ears.

We always had a lot to share
While I sat in the barber chair.

He'd ask if I were college bound
And talk of girls went round and round.

A small-town barber has a way
Of knowing what goes on each day.
Believes 'bout half of what he hears
While using scissors, comb, and shears.

From boy to man and in between
We two would view the changing scene.
I sure enjoyed his company
And barber shop philosophy.

One day he'll pack his tools away
And take a well-earned holiday.
He'll find himself an easy chair,
And someone else will cut my hair.

Now fifty years have come and gone
With hair cut short and hair left long.
My black hair now is silver gray
When it is cut on Saturday.

But Saturdays will never be
The same without his chemistry.
He's left me treasured souvenirs,
The man with scissors, comb, and shears.

50 YEARS AGO

SURRENDER. USS *Missouri,* Tokyo Bay. General Douglas MacArthur signs official documents as Lieutenant General Jonathan Wainwright and Lieutenant General A. E. Percival watch from behind. U.S. Navy Photograph, Courtesy of the National Archives.

PEACE BRINGS WORLDWIDE REJOICING

As peace broke out today—in all its glory, complexity, promise, and responsibility—the United Nations moved swiftly to formalize the Japanese surrender and to occupy the enemy homeland.

At the present moment, relations between the Allied powers and Japan are in a state of truce. This will continue for several days until General Douglas MacArthur, who has been named supreme commander for all Allied forces in the Far East,

can accept a written Japanese surrender on the basis of the Potsdam declaration.

Immediately after the news of the surrender decision was flashed to the world last night, General MacArthur sent word to the Japanese authorities instructing them to send a representative to Manila to arrange for the formal act of capitulation.

Today he dispatched a second note ordering the Nipponese envoy to fly in an all-white plane decorated with green crosses. With a sense of poetic justice, General MacArthur told the Japanese to use the code word "Bataan" for all communications between the envoy and American forces.

The surrender plane will leave Kyushu Island on Friday morning and will fly to an American airport on Ie Shima, a short distance from Okinawa. Six hours' advance notice of exact departure time and route must be given. From Ie Shima, an American plane will carry the surrender party to Manila.

General MacArthur warned the Japanese that the envoy must bring competent Army, Navy, and Air Force advisers with him and must bear credentials enabling him to represent Emperor Hirohito.

In Manila, it is assumed that the Japanese delegation will receive instructions regarding the technical details of the Allied occupation and similar problems. The surrender party is expected to return at once to Tokyo after conferring with General MacArthur to ensure that Allied orders are put into effect. It seems to be the consensus of most authorities that Allied military forces will begin to move into Japan, at least in token form, no later than early next week.

PEACE. Italian-American neighborhood, New York, New York.
Photo Courtesy of the National Archives.

Simultaneous statements in the four great Allied capitals—Washington, London, Moscow, and Chungking—shortly after 7:00 p.m. Eastern War Time yesterday disclosed that Japan had accepted the Allied surrender terms.

In Washington, President Truman added a sobering note to the great wave of thanksgiving and joyous emotion that swept the Allied world. "We are faced with the greatest task we ever have been faced with," the president said. "The emergency is as great as it was on December 7, 1941."

Emperor Hirohito told the Japanese people in a radiocast this morning that the Japanese Empire had been completely and irrevocably defeated. The emperor said he had been compelled to accept the Allied surrender stipulations in order to save the nation from "obliteration." In a concession both to military truth and the "face-saving" so dear to the Japanese mentality, he attributed his country's plight mainly to the atomic bomb—"a new and most cruel weapon, the power of which to do damage is incalculable."

General MacArthur was formally designated supreme commander for the Allied powers to accept the Japanese surrender.

The Japanese government, in a message sent through Switzerland, was instructed to end hostilities at once and to send emissaries to General MacArthur. Allied armed forces were ordered to halt offensive operations.

Today and tomorrow were proclaimed holidays, with V-J Day awaiting the signing of the formal surrender.

Everywhere throughout the world today, except in the former Axis countries, there was rejoicing and enthusiastic planning for the future. Britain's elation was summed up by Prime Minister Clement R. Attlee in a victory radiocast last night. "Our gratitude goes out to all our splendid allies, and above all to the United States without whose prodigious efforts this war in the East still would have many years to run," the prime minister declared. Mr. Attlee designated today and tomorrow as holidays in Britain.

In Canada, Prime Minister Mackenzie King proclaimed today V-J Day and said that next Sunday would be a day of prayer and thanksgiving. In countries worldwide, this day has become the day that will never, never be forgotten.

Originally printed in The Christian Science Monitor, *August 15, 1945.*

Bandstand
IN THE

Edward C. Colwell

I like to stroll down mem'ry lane
To days my childhood knew,
Though sure am I the past is gone
Forever from my view.

I linger here and there awhile
To just survey the scenes;
And through the haze of bygone days,
I travel back in dreams.

I walk along familiar roads
In daylight and in dark
Until I'm standing there beside
The bandstand in the park.

It wasn't really long ago
But just another day
When folks would come from miles around
To hear the town band play,

Park

To hear the tunes that helped us through
The lonely years of war
And made this nation with each peace
Rise greater than before.

Then change they would to gentler tunes
And songs of love's old story;
As melancholy silence fell,
The band played "Annie Laurie."

They've nearly vanished from the scene,
But sure they've left their mark
In hearts and minds of many folk—
The bandstands in the park.

Quiet Moments

Carolyn J. Tinkle

I love the quiet moments
    On a sultry, summer day.
We sit together watching
    How the lofty branches sway.

The sun is slowly setting,
    And the frogs their croaks they've found.
The noise of the cicadas
    Sounds like songs sung in the round.

Our children's happy laughter
    Can be heard around the bend,
Hurrying to finish games
    Before the day must end.

I savor quiet moments
    That I love to spend with you
Because, it seems, in the rush of things,
    They are so very few.

I love the quiet moments
    On a sultry, summer day.
Please let there be more quiet
    Time together, Lord, I pray.

Lawn Care Lamentations

Mike Exinger

Americans buy more than 200,000 push-reel mowers a year. I bought mine a few years ago when that number was only half what it is today. Of course, there are still four-hundred-gazillion gas-powered mowers in existence, most of which pass by my bedroom window at eight o'clock on weekend mornings. But the push mower is experiencing a renaissance—for a few good reasons.

ECOLOGY

Ecology, for one. Not only do push mowers not require gasoline (and not emit exhaust), but they're quieter, too. They supposedly give your grass a healthier cut (although how your grass can tell is beyond me), and the clippings are finer, giving a good source of renewable energy back to the lawn. You can also bag your clippings, but I gave that up after I lost my bagger a few years back as I was rounding the curve near the hedges.

The push mower is also a simple machine, which is really good for me, being a simple kind of guy. I'm not mechanically inclined, or even tilted, so not having to maintain another engine is quite a relief. (I used to own a Corvair.)

My mower only needs a once-a-year sharpening and a little oiling. But this isn't really why I own a push mower. I wanted a power mower, but my wife announced, "We are getting a push mower because we are fat." She weighs 125 pounds, so it was easy to see which one of us she meant.

EXERCISE

I must admit, our push mower is a great exercise program. I can burn off up to four hundred calories in an hour of lawn mowing, and I never have to watch a modern version of Jack LaLanne doing overly enthusiastic jumping jacks.

SOCIAL STANDING

Besides the exercise, the push-reel mower is a great attention grabber. I used to be known as "the guy who owns the Corvair." Now I'm known as "the guy with the old push mower." I feel I'm really making headway in the neighborhood social swirl.

My next-door neighbor's power mower has broken down. Now he comes over once a week to borrow my old-fashioned push mower. I receive great pleasure watching him push it back and forth across his lawn. And he really could use the exercise.

If you're thinking about making the switch, I have a couple of suggestions: Remember your high school physics class? Specifically the part about "for every action there is a reaction" and "bodies in motion tend to stay in motion"? Sticks in your lawn can get caught in the mower's blades, an action that stops your motion rather suddenly. I've placed some padding around the handles.

And keep in mind that it's not called a push mower for nothing. No matter how much exercise you feel you (or your spouse) need, if you have a lawn the size of East Texas, you may want to reconsider getting a push mower. For you, maybe something that requires less actual pushing might be better.

Even I've considered giving up my push mower for something less strenuous. My wife, though, has made me promise to return the sheep.

The Home

Kay Hoffman

It need not be a fancy home
To please our latest whim;
The plainest home is beautiful
Where our love dwells within.

Where the family lives together
In a warm and caring way
And shares each other's burdens
Or little joys each day.

Where the children grow up happy
Because they know they're loved;
Where God is honored in the home
And prayers are sent above.

It matters not a mansion
Or a cottage that we own;
Every home is beautiful
Where love's the cornerstone.

BRICK COTTAGE WITH ENTRANCE GARDEN
Missouri
Gay Bumgarner

FRESH MINT. T. DelAmo/H. Armstrong Roberts.

Country CHRONICLE
Lansing Christman

PEPPERMINT MEMORIES

The summer creek is sometimes my store of enchantment. I follow it upstream and climb the trickling waterfalls as though I were climbing a shimmering stairway up the hills. I find a store of particular pleasure when I catch the strong but pleasant mint aroma emanating from the lovely green plants with pale purple blooms along the creek. Their intoxicating scent fills the air around me.

The aroma of peppermint takes me back to my boyhood and excursions to the Main Street candy store. My boyish eyes filled with anticipation as I looked at the striped sticks of peppermint candy. I always carefully surveyed the entire glass case before choosing one cherished piece of candy. My eyes roved over the lollipops, the lemon drops, the licorice sticks, and all the other colors and flavors of sweet confections. Almost every time, though, I finally chose a peppermint stick. Nothing could beat that crisp taste and wonderful smell.

Even today, my eyes fill with that same sort of wonder as I push through the beds of peppermint that display their lush growth and blooms along the banks of the stream.

As I walk along the creek's edge, I cherish the fragrance of the plant that has found nourishment in the crevices and around the stones.

The plant has found its place in the shadow of rocks that once were pounded by ice and turned over and over by the turbulent flow from spring thaws.

Peppermint garnishes the beauty of this valley of the uplands. Here is a spear of bloom in the summer sun deep in the channel through the hills. Here is the mint, filling a basin of the earth where the strong fingers of water had carved curving and winding grooves through the slopes.

It is good that pleasurable things like peppermint come in a placid time of the year when water is a little more than a liquid carol, a cooling carol that goes well with the goldfinch's song over the hot summer fields. I relish the aroma of peppermint that fills the air when I walk out into the store of the hills for a sprig of peppermint and a song.

The author of two published books, Lansing Christman has been contributing to Ideals *for more than twenty years. Mr. Christman has also been published in several American, foreign, and braille anthologies. He lives in rural South Carolina.*

The House with Nobody in It

Joyce Kilmer

Whenever I walk to Suffern along the Erie track,
    I go by a poor old farmhouse with its shingles broken and black.
I suppose I've passed it a hundred times, but I always stop for a minute
    And look at the house, the tragic house, the house with nobody in it.

I have never seen a haunted house, but I hear there are such things;
    That they hold the talk of spirits, their mirth and sorrowings.
I know this house isn't haunted, and I wish it were, I do;
    For it wouldn't be so lonely if it had a ghost or two.

This house on the road to Suffern needs a dozen panes of glass,
    And somebody ought to weed the walk and take a scythe to the grass.
It needs new paint and shingles, and the vines should be trimmed and tied;
    But what it needs the most of all is some people living inside.

If I had a lot of money and all my debts were paid,
    I'd put a gang of men to work with brush and saw and spade.
I'd buy that place and fix it up the way it used to be,
    And I'd find some people who wanted a home and give it to them free.

Now, a new house standing empty, with staring window and door,
    Looks idle, perhaps, and foolish, like a hat on its block in the store.
But there's nothing mournful about it; it cannot be sad and lone
    For the lack of something within it that it has never known.

But a house that has done what a house should do, a house that has sheltered life,
    That has put its loving, wooden arms around a man and his wife,
A house that has echoed a baby's laugh and held up his stumbling feet,
    Is the saddest sight, when it's left alone, that ever your eyes could meet.

So whenever I go to Suffern along the Erie track,
    I never go by the empty house without stopping and looking back.
Yet it hurts me to look at the crumbling roof and the shutters fallen apart,
    For I can't help thinking the poor old house is a house with a broken heart.

ABANDONED HOMESTEAD
Minnesota
Bob Firth/International Stock

Weeding

Sylvia Trent Auxier

This weed spreads playful stems along the grass
As romping kittens, watchful, curl and wait;
Above its clean-carved leaves my swift hands pass,
Poise for its picking—waver, hesitate.

"Next time," I say; but when I weed again,
It holds pale flowers close in the elbowed nook
Of leaf and stem, and four green spurlets fan
The yielding air. I kneel and look and look.

The blooming's done, but now its hastate leaf
With flashing hilt of red allures the eye
From seeds asleep within an auburn sheaf
That points a slender finger at the sky.

Leaving its fast-maturing seeds intact,
I gaze upon its beauty and depart.
I'll gladly pay the price the years exact
For a tender, foolish, beauty-loving heart.

From My Garden Journal
by Deana Deck

CLEMATIS

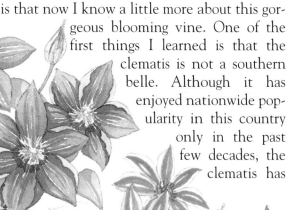

Shortly after moving to the mid-South nearly twenty years ago, I discovered the local botanical garden and took to exploring its myriad pathways. One day I strolled up a curving trail and encountered a lovely, rustic Victorian gazebo covered with the most amazing vine. I hadn't the faintest idea what it was. Until that time I had only gardened in the upper Midwest and upstate New York, so I assumed the plant in question was a southern native. It was late in the season, and a great number of seed pods had formed, but the plant was still blooming quite profusely. I gathered a handful of seeds and went to the head gardener's office to find out the name of this exotic wonder. It was, of course, a clematis.

I fell in love that day, and my attachment has grown stronger over the years. The difference is that now I know a little more about this gorgeous blooming vine. One of the first things I learned is that the clematis is not a southern belle. Although it has enjoyed nationwide popularity in this country only in the past few decades, the clematis has

been around a lot longer in Europe and Great Britain. One of the first known references to the British native C. *vitalba* was in a book of herbals published in 1548. In 1569, a Spanish native, C. *Vitella*, was introduced to English gardens, where it soon became known as "Virgin's Bower" in honor of Queen Elizabeth I.

It was not until 1958, when British plant breeder George Jackman crossed three species to create the deep purple hybrid C. *x jackmanii*, that clematis breeding really caught on. Now some 230 species are widely distributed throughout the temperate regions of the world, with one hundred hybrid species being grown commercially in America. In addition, species have been found growing wild in just about every climate region on the planet.

No matter where you live in this country, there is a clematis variety that will grow in your garden—even in the chilly regions of upper Montana, North Dakota, Minnesota, Wisconsin, Maine, and Vermont. The hardiest clematis for cold-weather climates are the *Clematis integrifolia*, or Solitary Clematis, and the Ground Clematis, C. *recta*. Clematis vines bless us with an extremely long blooming season. Even the early bloomers will often reward the gardener with an encore in September.

The ultimate cottage garden flower, clematis can be easily trained to grow up a wall and around a window or doorway; and unlike some forms of ivy, it won't sink air roots deep into minute spaces in mortar, brick, or siding, which can cause substantial damage to structures. Although clematis will grow along a rough surface without the aid of a trellis, the vine is easier to control if you provide it with some support. In the South, a trellis is essential to provide the air circulation between the plant and wall that helps prevent the scourge of humid climates, powdery mildew.

Clematis differs from many other climbing vines in that it doesn't actually produce tendrils, nor does the vine itself twine around its support. Instead the vine grows fairly straight, but leaves that encounter a possible support transform their stems into a curly tendril that will cling tenaciously. In fact, when attempting to retrain a wayward vine that is headed in the wrong direction, it is often easier simply to cut these tendril-like leaves than to unwind them.

The one major idiosyncrasy of the clematis is that it wants its head in the sun and its feet in the cool shade. This condition can best be accomplished by planting a low-growing ground cover like vinca at the base of the plant or by protecting the roots with a thick layer of compost, leaf mold, or shredded bark. A two-inch layer of pebbles will protect the roots and permit the passage of water. Small slabs of stone spaced far enough from the main stem to permit moisture to penetrate the soil will also keep the soil cool.

In general, the best location for clematis is on the eastern side of a structure. It will receive adequate sunlight, the roots will be shaded in the heat of a summer afternoon, and the delicate vines will be somewhat protected from strong westerly winds.

In a cold climate, a south-facing wall is better for the plant than a similar wall in the Sunbelt. Clematis can survive and bloom quite nicely with only a half day of sunlight, but it cannot do well in the dry soil that is characteristic of gardens with a southern exposure.

There is a misconception that clematis must have an alkaline soil to thrive. This is because some of the species native to England do best in limestone or chalky soil. Most popular garden clematis do quite well in neutral or even slightly acidic soil.

Feeding clematis is a simple matter if the soil has been properly amended. The most important feeding is in the fall. It should consist of a thick layer of composted manure that is placed around the base of the plant but at least five inches from the stems to prevent damage. This compost layer will also serve as a winter mulch.

One of the most common questions regarding clematis is how and when to prune them. To understand this, it's important to know something about their growth and blooming habits. Several species bloom only on old growth. Therefore, pruning should be light and should be done immediately following blooming. Many other species bloom on current season growth which springs from old wood. If pruning is required for appearance, therefore, old wood should be cut back only to a point at which healthy buds are still visible. Often the lower portions of these vines will no longer be producing shoots, and cutting them back too drastically can result in no blooms at all. The third type plant, which blooms in very late summer and early autumn, blooms on new or current season growth only and can be pruned completely back to a height of two to three feet in February or March.

A basic rule of thumb regarding pruning is that species that bloom before the end of June are blooming on old wood and should be trimmed back sparingly, if at all. Those that bloom in July or later are blooming on current season wood and can be pruned more heavily.

With basic care, clematis will flourish on the windows or trellises of your home, and you may develop your own strong attachment to this gorgeous blooming vine.

Deana Deck lives in Nashville, Tennessee, where her popular garden column is a regular feature in The Tennessean.

She Planted Beauty

Mary E. Linton

Out here in this wild, lonely spot
    Beyond the city's farthest edge,
Which some say even God forgot,
    A small, pink rose still keeps its pledge.

I found it in among the weeds—
    A bit of beauty planted here
By someone long ago whose needs
    Were crying out for beauty near.

Beyond, where vines for years have run
    (I had not noticed it before),
A stone foundation—home of one
    Who planted roses by her door.

Oh, I shall never know her name
    Nor why she finally went away,
But in her soul there was the same
    Wild song that sings in mine today.

Though she may know a greater sphere
    Beyond the universe's edge,
I know her spirit lingers here
    Where one pink rose still keeps its pledge.

SINGLE ROSE
Charles Boorland/F-Stock Inc.

CASCADE OF ROSES
La Habra, California
Kristen Olenick/F-Stock Inc.

I Wrapped Summer's Ending

Loise Pinkerton Fritz

I wrapped summer's ending
With work-a-day chores;
I dusted the garden
And swept its earth floor.

I picked ripened grapes,
All bunched on the vine,
And gathered the pine cones
From under the pines.

With basket in hand
I harvested gourds,
Ripe sunflower seeds,
And apples to store.

I wrapped summer's ending
With happy-time days
Then gave thanks to God
And tied it with praise.

DAYLILIES ON A SUMMER DAY
Bristol, New Hampshire
William Johnson
Johnson's Photography

Readers' Forum

Meet Our Ideals Readers and Their Families

"Togetherness" is what Great-grandma CARRIE JENKINS wanted to subtitle this picture of Kelsey and Eric Tomlinson. Kelsey, age four, demonstrates her love and affection for her baby brother Eric, a welcome addition to the family. At age two, he has already impressed his great-grandma by changing the videotapes in the VCR!

Both Kelsey and Eric enjoy the outdoors and take advantage of a big backyard in the summer months. They live in Akron, Ohio, only minutes from Carrie.

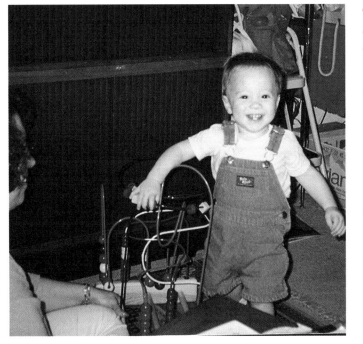

Grandma PEGGY WILLIAMSON of Lynchburg, Virginia, is very proud of little Marshall, her "sunbeam." The only child of Stacy and Ruth Williamson, Marshall is always, according to Grandma, a well-behaved child who loves clowns and posing for photographs! However, as Grandma notes, his fiery red hair is often difficult to tame.

Stacy, Ruth, and Marshall live in nearby Pamplin, Virginia, which allows for many frequent visits to Grandma's house.

CATHERINE ROBERTS of Troy, Michigan, sent *Ideals* this picture of her granddaughter, Rachael Ann Nowak, posing on the sofa. Although Rachael lives with her parents in Celina, Ohio, she spends several days a year with her grandparents in Michigan. Being the only granddaughter in the family, Rachael, age two and a half, is doted on by everyone. Catherine told us that Rachael loves attention, and she really enjoyed her "photo shoot."

ATTENTION *IDEALS* READERS: The *Ideals* editors are looking for "favorite memories" for the magazine. Please send a typed description of your favorite holiday memory or family tradition to: Favorite Memories, c/o Editorial Department, Ideals Publications Inc., P.O. Box 305300, Nashville, Tennessee 37230.

THANK YOU Carrie Jenkins, Peggy Williamson, and Catherine Roberts for sharing with *Ideals*. We hope to hear from other readers who would like to share photos and stories with the *Ideals* family. Please include a self-addressed, stamped envelope if you would like the photos returned. Keep your original photographs for safekeeping and send duplicate photos along with your name, address, and telephone number to:

READERS' FORUM
IDEALS PUBLICATIONS INC.
P.O. BOX 305300
NASHVILLE, TENNESSEE 37230

ideals

Publisher, Patricia A. Pingry
Editor, Lisa C. Thompson
Copy Editor, Michelle Prater Burke
Electronic Prepress Manager,
   Amilyn K. Lanning
Editorial Intern, Heather R. McArthur
Contributing Editors, Lansing Christman, Deana Deck, Russ Flint, Pamela Kennedy, Patrick McRae, Mary Skarmeas, Nancy Skarmeas

ACKNOWLEDGMENTS

DOORBELLS by Rachel Field. Reprinted by permission of the author's estate. THE GAIN from *ALL IN A LIFETIME* by Edgar A. Guest, copyright © 1938 by the Reilly & Lee Co. Reprinted by permission of the author's estate. SHE PLANTED BEAUTY from *ON WINGS OF THE SOUL* by Mary E. Linton. Reprinted by permission of the author's estate. TUMBLE-DOWN COTTAGE from *SILVER LININGS* by Patience Strong, copyright © 1939, published by Frederick Muller Ltd. Reprinted by permission of Rupert Crew Limited. Our sincere thanks to the following authors whom we were unable to contact: Sylvia Trent Auxier for WEEDING from *MEADOW-RUE*, copyright © 1948 by The Decker Press, and Helen Morgan Brooks for PLANS.

ANNOUNCING A NEW AND UNIQUE PUBLICATION FROM IDEALS
FIRST LADIES OF THE WHITE HOUSE

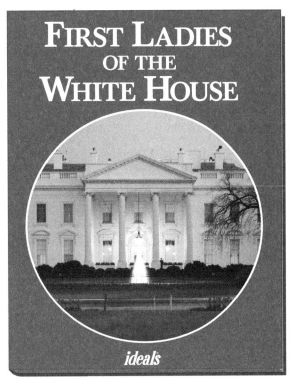

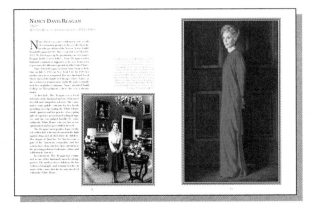

First Ladies of the White House tells the stories of the women who supported our presidents. From Martha Washington to Hillary Rodham Clinton, each woman defined her role in a unique way, and each made a lasting contribution to the history of our nation.

OFFICIAL PORTRAITS AND FAMILY PHOTOGRAPHS
In this full-color, eighty-page volume, Ideals has paired biographies of each first lady with portraits, paintings, engravings, and drawings of the women and their families. Each of the presidents' wives is featured, as well as the many official White House hostesses—nieces, daughters, and friends—who filled the role of first lady for a bachelor or widower president.

BEHIND-THE-SCENES LOOK AT PRESIDENTIAL LIFE
Each of our first ladies has faced the difficult task of filling a role that is neither elected nor appointed yet comes complete with a full range of public responsibilities and expectations. Some first ladies embraced the role with confidence and ambition, like Sarah Polk (who believed that she, along with her husband, was chosen to lead the American nation and took a full share of the work of the presidency) or Eleanor Roosevelt (whose activism and energy redefined the role of first lady for all who would follow). Read also of the reluctant first ladies, like Martha Washington, who longed for retirement at Mount Vernon; or Bess Truman, who valued her family life and privacy above all else.

INSPIRATIONAL ROLE MODELS
The story of the first ladies is also a story of true partnerships; for many of our presidents owe their successes in large part to the support and hard work of their wives. But the true inspiration in these stories lies in the individual struggles of each woman to find peace and purpose in her position. In their personal histories are inspirational role models for all American women, men, and children.

A BOOK FOR THE WHOLE FAMILY
First Ladies of the White House is truly a volume to treasure, for those who remember some of these events and for those youngsters who wish to learn of them. All Americans who believe in the spirit of democracy upon which our nation was founded will cherish this special book.

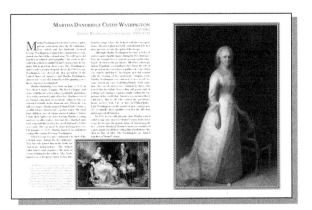